AF413512

SPIRITUAL INTEGRITY

NAVIGATING LIFE WITH MORAL COMPASSION

DR. MINAKSHI BANSAL

DEDICATION

This book is dedicated to all seekers of truth and authenticity—those who courageously venture into the depths of their own hearts to align their lives with their highest values. To my family, friends, and mentors, whose unwavering support and love have illuminated my path, this work is a testament to the power of our shared journey. May it inspire you as you have inspired me, guiding each step towards a life of profound integrity and compassion.

ϸϸϸ

Contents

Contents

Prayer

"Om Bhadram Karnebhih Shrinuyama Devah
Bhadram Pashyemakshabhiryajatrah
Sthirairangais Tushtuvamsastanubhih
Vyashema Devahitam Yadayuh
Svasti Na Indro Vriddhashravah
Svasti Nah Pusha Vishwavedah
Svasti Nastarkshyo Arishtanemih
Svasti No Brihaspatir Dadhatu
Om Shantih Shantih Shantih"

This mantra is a prayer for universal well-being, invoking the blessings of various deities for protection, health, and happiness. It emphasizes the importance of experiencing the auspicious through all senses and living a life aligned with divine purpose. The repetition of "Shantih" at the end signifies a deep desire for peace in the individual, the environment, and the universe at large. This mantra is often recited as a prayer for peace, prosperity, and the physical and spiritual well-being of all beings.

ᘯᘯᘯ

About The Author

Dr. Minakshi Bansal, born in the bustling metropolis of Delhi, India, has led a life steeped in artistry, scholarly pursuit, and an unwavering commitment to societal betterment. Following her marriage, she relocated to Ahmedabad, Gujarat, where she has since blossomed into a multifaceted beacon of inspiration for many. Dr. Minakshi is not only recognized as a gifted artist in the realm of Fine Arts but also as an esteemed author, a devoted social worker and a dedicated research scholar in Psychology. Her journey, marked by a profound dedication to elevating those around her, especially the downtrodden and underprivileged children of society, is a testament to her deep-seated belief in the transformative power of engagement and empathy.

From her earliest days, Minakshi was distinguished by an insatiable appetite for reading. Her literary universe was inhabited by characters and narratives that spanned ethical tales, motivational and inspirational stories, and the mythic parables imbued with life lessons. This voracious reading habit was not merely for personal edification but was driven by a desire to distill and disseminate the essence of these narratives to foster the development of students and peers alike. She was particularly captivated by the lives and teachings of historical figures and spiritual leaders such as Adi Shankaracharya, Swami Vivekananda, Dr. APJ Abdul Kalam, Mahamana Pandit Madan Mohan Malviya, Mahatma Gandhi, Sardar Vallabhai Patel, and Vinoba Bhave, among others. Their philosophies and life stories fueled her ambition to embody their ideals of resilience, selflessness, and relentless pursuit of knowledge.

Dr. Minakshi's academic and practical engagement with psychology has been equally noteworthy. As a research scholar, her focus has been on exploring the intricate tapestry of the human psyche, aiming to unlock the potential for psychological well-being and societal harmony. Her scholarly work is complemented by her active involvement in social work, where she employs her academic insights to make tangible differences in the lives of the underprivileged. Her endeavours in social work are characterized by an innovative approach that combines traditional wisdom with contemporary psychological practices to address the multifaceted challenges faced by these communities.

Her artistic talents, another facet of her diverse capabilities, are not merely a personal passion but also serve as a medium through which she communicates and connects with others. Her art, rich in symbolism and emotional depth, reflects her philosophical inquiries and social concerns, offering viewers a glimpse into the breadth of her intellect and the depth of her compassion.

In addition to her contributions to the arts and social sciences, Dr. Minakshi has embraced the healing arts of Pranic Healing, mastering the techniques developed by Master Choa Kok Sui. This practice, which focuses on the manipulation of Prana or life energy to heal the body and aura, has been both a personal journey of discovery and a means through which she extends her healing touch to others. Her proficiency in Pranic Healing is complemented by her advocacy and teaching of various forms of meditation aimed at rejuvenation, personal betterment, and the cultivation of harmony within individuals and communities alike.

Dr. Minakshi's life is a narrative of relentless pursuit, not just of personal achievement but of the upliftment and empowerment of society at large. Her diverse interests and talents—spanning the arts, literature, psychology, and the healing practices—converge on a singular path of service. She embodies the spirit of the luminaries who inspired her, channelling their legacy through her actions and teachings. Through her books, art, and social initiatives, she continues to inspire a new generation to embark on their own journeys of self-discovery, resilience, and altruism.

Her commitment to social betterment, particularly her focus on uplifting underprivileged children, reflects a deep understanding of the transformative potential of education and personal development. By integrating her knowledge of psychology, her artistic sensibilities, and her healing practices, Dr. Bansal has developed a holistic approach to social work that addresses both the immediate needs and the long-term well-being of the communities she serves.

As an author, Dr. Minakshi's writings offer a blend of inspirational insights, practical wisdom, and reflective contemplations drawn from her extensive reading and life experiences. Her books serve as a guide for those seeking to navigate the complexities of life with grace, resilience, and purpose. Through her narratives, she extends an invitation to her readers to explore the depths of their own potential and to contribute meaningfully to the collective well-being of society.

In Dr. Minakshi Bansal, we find a remarkable synthesis of the artist, the scholar, the healer, and the social activist. Her life's work stands as a beacon of hope and a source of inspiration for individuals seeking to make a difference in the world. Her story is a compelling reminder of the power of individual action, rooted in compassion and driven by a profound commitment to the betterment of humanity. Dr. Minakshi's legacy is not just in the tangible outcomes of her efforts but in the enduring spirit of inquiry, empathy, and service that she embodies.

ᏭᏭᏭ

Preface

In the vast expanse of human experience, few quests are as profound and challenging as the pursuit of spiritual integrity. This journey, which intertwines the threads of ethical conduct and spiritual growth, invites each of us to explore deep realms of personal transformation and to embrace a way of living that resonates with our innermost values. It is a path marked by questions as much as answers, an exploration that goes beyond the surface of morality and into the essence of what it means to live truthfully and wholeheartedly.

At the heart of this exploration is the understanding that our spiritual and ethical selves are not isolated aspects of our being but are deeply connected and dynamically interactive. How we act in our everyday lives reflects our deepest spiritual commitments and, in turn, our spiritual practices deeply inform our choices and actions. This reciprocal relationship forms the core of spiritual integrity—a harmonious alignment between beliefs and behavior that fosters genuine peace and fulfillment.

The inspiration to write this book stemmed from my observations of the dissonance many people experience between their spiritual beliefs and their daily actions. Too often, there seems to be a disconnect that prevents the beautiful, life-affirming principles of spirituality from fully permeating everyday life. I have met many individuals who express a desire to live a more integrated life, one where their actions consistently reflect their spiritual values. This book is a response to that longing, an offering to anyone who seeks to bridge the gap between their spiritual aspirations and their real-world experiences.

In the pages that follow, we delve into the nuances of what it means to live with spiritual integrity. We examine the virtues that form the bedrock of this way of living—compassion, honesty, forgiveness, humility, and more—and explore practical ways to cultivate these qualities in the thick of daily life's challenges and routines. Each chapter is crafted to not only provide insights and reflections but also to offer actionable guidance that can be implemented immediately, bringing us closer to a life of coherence and grace.

The journey to spiritual integrity requires more than the passive consumption of ideas; it demands active engagement and a willingness to look inward. It challenges us to confront our shadows, to question our motives, and to consistently choose actions that align with our deepest truths. This process is not always easy. It can be fraught with discomfort and difficulty as it compels us to navigate the complexities of ethical dilemmas and to make choices that may go against the grain of mainstream culture or our habitual ways of being.

However, the rewards of such a journey are immeasurable. Living with spiritual integrity brings a profound sense of peace and confidence that comes from knowing one's life is in alignment with one's values. It strengthens relationships, builds trust and respect with others, and creates a stable foundation for facing life's inevitable challenges. Above all, it offers a deeper connection with the divine, the universe, or whatever higher power one believes in, enriching one's spiritual life in immeasurable ways.

This book is an invitation to embark on this transformative journey. It is meant for anyone, regardless of religious affiliation or spiritual background, who seeks to live a more authentic, ethical, and spiritually-aligned life. Whether you are well along your spiritual path or just beginning to explore what spirituality means to you, this book aims to support and guide you in deepening your practice of living according to your spiritual and ethical beliefs.

As you turn these pages, I encourage you to approach them with an open heart and a curious mind. Allow yourself the space to reflect on the concepts presented, to question them, and to see how they resonate with your personal experiences and beliefs. I hope that this book serves as a valuable resource on your journey, providing insight and inspiration that lead to greater clarity and commitment in your quest for spiritual integrity.

The pursuit of spiritual integrity is one of the most significant and rewarding adventures one can undertake. It offers each of us a pathway to become not only what we believe in but also what we aspire to be, in the deepest sense. It challenges us to rise above the mundane, to transcend our limitations, and to live in a way that brings light not only into our own lives but also into the world around us. Let us embark on this journey together, with courage and hope, as we navigate the intricate dance of ethics and spirituality that defines the essence of who we truly are.

Dr. Minakshi Bansal
Social Activist
Ahmedabad, Gujarat, Bharat

ᐅᐅᐅ

ONE

THE FOUNDATIONS OF SPIRITUAL INTEGRITY

Spiritual integrity is a profound concept that involves maintaining consistency between one's values, beliefs, and actions. At its core, it requires a commitment to living truthfully in accordance with one's spiritual and moral beliefs, forming a cornerstone for a life filled with purpose and meaning. This foundational principle encourages individuals to reflect deeply on their ethical commitments and spiritual practices, ensuring that these elements are not only harmoniously aligned but also actively guide their daily actions and decisions.

The journey towards spiritual integrity begins with self-awareness. It is essential for individuals to engage in introspective practices that help them understand their core values and beliefs. Meditation, reflective journaling, and thoughtful dialogue with others can serve as effective tools in this pursuit. Through these practices, one can gain clarity about what truly matters to them, which in turn informs their moral compass.

Another key aspect of establishing spiritual integrity is authenticity. This involves being genuine in one's expressions and actions, and not merely conforming to external expectations or societal norms. Authenticity requires courage and vulnerability, as it often entails showing one's true self, with all its imperfections and strengths. By embracing authenticity, individuals can foster deeper connections with others and with the divine, enhancing their spiritual journey.

Ethics and spirituality are deeply intertwined, as ethical behavior is often seen as a manifestation of one's spiritual beliefs. To live with spiritual integrity, one must strive to act ethically in all aspects of life. This includes being honest, just, and compassionate, and treating all beings with respect and dignity. Ethical behavior reinforces spiritual development, as it aligns one's actions with their spiritual ideals, creating a unified and purposeful life.

Cultivating a Practice of Continuous Reflection

To maintain spiritual integrity, continuous reflection is crucial. Life is dynamic, and as individuals grow and encounter new experiences, their understanding of themselves and their spiritual beliefs may evolve. Regular reflection helps individuals to reassess their values and practices, ensuring they remain relevant and aligned with their current life circumstances. This ongoing process not only deepens one's spiritual understanding but also reinforces their commitment to living an ethical life.

Community plays a significant role in supporting and enhancing one's spiritual integrity. Engaging with a community of like-minded individuals can provide encouragement, guidance, and a sense of belonging. Community interactions can also present opportunities to practice and refine one's ethical and spiritual commitments through collaborative activities and shared rituals.

In essence, the foundations of spiritual integrity are built on a deep commitment to living a life that is true to one's spiritual and ethical values. This commitment must be nurtured through continuous self-awareness, authentic living, ethical conduct, regular reflection, and community engagement. By firmly establishing these foundations, individuals can lead a spiritually fulfilling life, marked by a profound sense of inner peace and purpose. Through the daily practice of spiritual integrity, one not only benefits personally but also contributes positively to the broader community, fostering a more compassionate and ethical world.

ᐅᐅᐅ

"True spiritual integrity arises when our actions not only align with our beliefs but when they also elevate our very essence. Every decision is a reflection of who we aspire to be, a step toward the divine."

ᐅᐅᐅ

TWO

VIRTUES OF THE HEART: CULTIVATING COMPASSION AND KINDNESS

Cultivating compassion and kindness is central to spiritual growth and ethical development. These virtues, often referred to as the "virtues of the heart," are the driving force behind a life that radiates warmth, empathy, and understanding. Compassion is the ability to feel deep empathy for the suffering of others, while kindness is the act of extending care and goodwill towards them. Together, these virtues create a harmonious and loving approach to life that can transform individuals and their communities.

Compassion begins with the ability to see beyond oneself and recognize the experiences and emotions of others. It requires a willingness to connect with the feelings and struggles of those around us, whether they are close friends, family members, or strangers. This connection involves not just understanding but also a sense of shared humanity, acknowledging that everyone has their own burdens and challenges. Compassionate individuals often find themselves drawn to acts of service and support, seeking to alleviate the suffering they encounter.

Kindness, on the other hand, is the outward expression of compassion. It manifests in small acts of goodwill, thoughtful gestures, and a general attitude of helpfulness. Kindness is not merely about grand gestures; it is about the everyday moments when we choose to treat others with respect and care. A kind word, a listening ear, or a helping hand can make a significant difference in someone's life. The beauty of kindness is that it often has a ripple effect, inspiring others to act with similar generosity and warmth.

These virtues are closely tied to the concept of spiritual integrity. Living with compassion and kindness requires consistency in one's values and actions. It means being aware of the impact our behavior has on others and striving to align our actions with our ethical and spiritual beliefs. This alignment fosters trust and respect, both within oneself and with others, creating a sense of harmony and peace.

An essential aspect of cultivating compassion and kindness is developing a nonjudgmental mindset. When we release the need to judge others based on their appearances, beliefs, or behaviors, we open ourselves to a broader understanding of the world. This shift in perspective allows for a greater capacity for empathy and acceptance. By letting go of judgment, we can focus on supporting and uplifting those around us, creating an environment where kindness can flourish.

Another key to fostering these virtues is practicing gratitude. Gratitude helps us appreciate the positive aspects of life and recognize the goodness in others. When we approach life with a grateful heart, we are more inclined to be compassionate and kind. This mindset encourages us to value relationships, cherish the present moment, and embrace the beauty in everyday interactions.

Developing compassion and kindness also involves cultivating self-compassion. Before we can extend these virtues to others, we must first learn to be gentle and forgiving with ourselves. Self-compassion involves acknowledging our own struggles, embracing our imperfections, and treating ourselves with the same care and kindness we offer to others. This inner compassion creates a solid foundation from which we can genuinely connect with others and support them in their journey.

To nurture compassion and kindness, it is helpful to engage in practices that promote mindfulness and presence. Mindfulness allows us to be fully present in each moment, which enhances our ability to connect with others and understand their needs. Through mindfulness practices such as meditation and deep breathing, we can quiet the noise of daily life and focus on the people and situations that matter most. This heightened awareness leads to a greater capacity for compassion and kindness in our interactions.

The virtues of the heart, compassion, and kindness are transformative forces that have the power to change lives. By cultivating these virtues, we can create a world where empathy, understanding, and generosity are valued and celebrated. As we embrace these virtues, we not only strengthen our own spiritual journey but also contribute to a more compassionate and kinder society. Ultimately, the practice of compassion and kindness is a lifelong journey that invites us to grow, connect, and share our love and warmth with the world.

ppp

"Compassion is the thread that weaves through the fabric of a fulfilled life; it connects us to others through the shared experience of humanity. By extending kindness, we receive a deeper understanding of ourselves and our purpose."

❦❦❦

THREE

THE ROLE OF HONESTY IN SPIRITUAL PRACTICE

Honesty is a fundamental virtue in the quest for spiritual growth and integrity. It serves as the foundation for building trust in relationships, deepening one's self-awareness, and maintaining a clear conscience. In the context of spiritual practice, honesty is not just about telling the truth to others but also about being true to oneself. This dual aspect of honesty is crucial for anyone seeking to live a spiritually aligned life.

At the heart of spiritual honesty is the commitment to authenticity. This means being genuine in thoughts, words, and actions, and avoiding any form of deceit or pretense. By embracing authenticity, individuals can ensure that their external behaviors are in harmony with their internal beliefs and values. This congruence is essential for cultivating a sense of peace and integrity, which are key components of spiritual well-being.

One of the most challenging aspects of practicing honesty in one's spiritual journey is self-honesty. This involves a rigorous examination of one's thoughts, motivations, and actions to ensure they align with personal and spiritual goals. Self-honesty requires courage, as it often entails confronting uncomfortable truths about oneself. However, this practice is vital for personal growth and spiritual development, as it helps individuals identify areas where they may be falling short of their ideals and provides an opportunity for improvement.

Honesty also plays a critical role in interpersonal relationships within a spiritual context. Open and truthful communication fosters trust and understanding between individuals, which are necessary for building supportive and nurturing spiritual communities. When people feel they can trust each other to be honest, they are more likely to share their true thoughts and feelings, which enhances mutual support and empathy. This openness not only strengthens individual relationships but also contributes to the overall health and vibrancy of the spiritual community.

Moreover, honesty has a profound impact on ethical behavior. Ethical dilemmas often arise in daily life, and having a solid foundation of honesty helps individuals make decisions that are not only legally or socially acceptable but also spiritually congruent. Honesty guides people in choosing actions that reflect their highest moral and spiritual aspirations, thereby avoiding behaviors that could lead to guilt, regret, or moral conflict.

Navigating Challenges with Honesty

Maintaining honesty can be challenging, especially when faced with situations where truth-telling might lead to conflict or discomfort. In such cases, it is essential to balance honesty with tact and compassion. Speaking the truth in a kind and considerate manner can mitigate potential harm and ensure that the message is received in a constructive way. This approach not only upholds the virtue of honesty but also respects the feelings and dignity of others.

Another challenge in practicing honesty is dealing with the fear of judgment or rejection. Often, individuals may choose to hide the truth or present a façade to fit in or please others. Overcoming this fear is crucial for maintaining spiritual integrity. By fostering self-acceptance and cultivating a supportive spiritual environment, individuals can feel more secure in being honest about their true selves.

Incorporating honesty into daily spiritual practices can also enhance mindfulness and presence. For example, engaging in honest self-reflection during meditation or journaling can deepen one's understanding of their spiritual path and clarify their intentions. These practices encourage a mindful awareness of one's thoughts and actions, reinforcing the commitment to live authentically.

Honesty is indispensable in the pursuit of spiritual integrity. It enriches personal growth, strengthens relationships, and upholds ethical standards. By embracing honesty in both personal and communal aspects of life, individuals can build a spiritually fulfilling existence that not only nurtures their own well-being but also contributes positively to the world around them. The pursuit of honesty is a lifelong journey that requires vigilance, courage, and compassion, but the rewards of living a truthful and authentic life are immeasurable.

ᏜᏜᏜ

"Honesty is more than truth-telling; it is the foundation of a life lived authentically. It demands courage to reveal one's true self, but in this vulnerability lies our greatest strength."

ϷϷϷ

FOUR

FORGIVENESS: A PATH TO INNER PEACE

Forgiveness is a powerful and transformative aspect of spiritual practice that promotes healing, peace, and reconciliation. It involves letting go of resentment and grudges against those who have caused us harm, whether intentionally or unintentionally. The practice of forgiveness is not just about absolving others; it also encompasses forgiving oneself, which can be equally challenging. Embracing forgiveness leads to emotional liberation and a deeper sense of inner peace, essential elements for spiritual growth.

The journey of forgiveness begins with understanding its true nature. Forgiveness does not imply condoning wrong behavior or forgetting the hurt caused. Instead, it is about releasing the burden of anger and bitterness that binds us to past injuries. This release allows individuals to reclaim their peace of mind and move forward in life with a lighter heart. Forgiveness is a gift to oneself, a crucial step in healing and spiritual evolution.

One of the significant challenges in practicing forgiveness is overcoming the initial feelings of injustice and betrayal. These emotions are natural responses to being wronged, but dwelling on them can lead to a cycle of anger and retaliation that harms all involved. Recognizing that forgiveness is primarily for one's own well-being can be a helpful perspective. It is not about altering the past or changing others but about transforming one's own emotional state and life experience.

Self-Forgiveness: Healing from Within

Forgiving oneself is an essential aspect of the forgiveness process. Self-forgiveness involves addressing the guilt, shame, or regret that one may carry from past mistakes or poor decisions. Like forgiveness of others, self-forgiveness is not about excusing one's errors but rather about accepting them and committing to personal growth. This acceptance is crucial for maintaining mental and spiritual health, as unresolved self-blame can lead to chronic stress, depression, or self-sabotage.

Practicing self-forgiveness can be challenging, particularly if one holds a perfectionist or overly critical view of oneself. It requires compassion and understanding that everyone makes mistakes and that errors are opportunities for learning and growth. Developing a supportive self-dialogue that encourages acceptance and compassion is key to fostering self-forgiveness.

The Role of Empathy in Forgiveness

Empathy plays a vital role in the ability to forgive others. By trying to understand the perspectives and circumstances of those who have wronged us, we can often find reasons to mitigate our anger. Empathy involves seeing beyond our pain and recognizing the shared human vulnerabilities that lead to mistakes and wrongful actions. This broader perspective can soften our judgments and open the door to forgiveness.

Moreover, empathy not only facilitates forgiveness but also promotes deeper connections and trust within relationships. It encourages a culture of openness and understanding, where individuals feel safe to express their faults and vulnerabilities without fear of harsh judgment.

Rituals and Practices to Encourage Forgiveness

Engaging in specific rituals and practices can aid in the process of forgiveness. Meditation, prayer, and guided visualizations focused on forgiveness can help calm the mind and foster the emotional strength needed to let go of grudges. Writing exercises, such as composing forgiveness letters (even if they are never sent), can be therapeutic. These practices allow individuals to express their feelings constructively and reflect on the forgiveness process.

Community support can also be invaluable in fostering forgiveness. Sharing one's experiences and challenges with forgiving within a supportive group setting can provide insights and encouragement. Witnessing others in their forgiveness journeys can inspire and motivate individuals to pursue their own paths to forgiveness.

Living with Forgiveness

Adopting a lifestyle that embraces forgiveness can have profound spiritual and psychological benefits. Individuals who practice forgiveness report lower levels of anxiety and stress and higher feelings of hope and happiness. Forgiveness enriches one's spiritual life by aligning actions with compassionate values, leading to a more harmonious existence.

Forgiveness is a dynamic and powerful practice that facilitates emotional and spiritual healing. It requires courage, empathy, and persistence but yields a rewarding path to inner peace and personal growth. By incorporating forgiveness into daily life, individuals open themselves to a world of renewed possibilities and deeper spiritual connections. The practice of forgiveness not only heals the wounds of the past but also paves the way for a future filled with peace, joy, and spiritual fulfillment.

ᐁᐁᐁ

"Forgiveness is the key that unlocks the chains of bitterness. When we forgive, we free ourselves from the weight of past grievances and open our hearts to healing and peace."

ppp

FIVE

HUMILITY: THE QUIET STRENGTH

Humility is often misunderstood as a sign of weakness or a lack of confidence, but in reality, it is a profound strength that underpins much spiritual and ethical development. True humility involves recognizing one's own limitations and imperfections, and being open to learning and growth. It is about understanding one's place in the broader context of the world, acknowledging that one is not the center of the universe, and respecting the value and contributions of others.

The Essence of Humility

At its core, humility is the antithesis of ego. It is the quality of being modest and respectful, without seeking the spotlight or demanding recognition for one's achievements. Humble individuals do not think less of themselves; they simply think of themselves less, focusing more on the needs and successes of others. This orientation towards the collective rather than the individual can lead to deeper relationships, better teamwork, and a more compassionate society.

Humility also involves a realistic self-assessment of one's abilities and achievements. It includes acknowledging when help is needed and when others know more or can perform better in certain areas. This realistic, unbiased self-assessment is crucial not only in personal development but also in nurturing a supportive and truthful environment whether at work, in family, or within communities.

Humility and Spiritual Growth

In many spiritual traditions, humility is seen as essential to spiritual growth. It is often the first step toward recognizing a higher power and one's dependence on that power. For instance, in many forms of meditation and prayer, practitioners humble themselves as a way of opening up to divine guidance. By lowering the ego, individuals make room for spiritual insights and transformations that might not otherwise surface.

Furthermore, humility can lead to increased self-awareness and emotional intelligence. By acknowledging their own faults and limitations, humble individuals are better able to manage their emotions and react to stressful situations with calmness and reason. They are also more likely to engage in moral and ethical behavior, as they are not blinded by their own self-importance.

The Role of Humility in Relationships

Humility fosters stronger and more resilient relationships. By prioritizing others' needs and recognizing their contributions, humble individuals build bonds of trust and respect. In conflicts, a humble approach can de-escalate tensions and facilitate compromise, as each party is more willing to admit their mistakes and be open to alternative points of view.

In leadership, humility is particularly powerful. Humble leaders are admired and respected, not feared. They are approachable, willing to listen, and open to feedback, which not only makes them effective managers but also role models for their teams. Their leadership style encourages an environment of continuous improvement and open communication, fostering innovation and commitment among their staff.

Challenges and Misconceptions of Humility

Despite its many benefits, humility can be challenging to practice consistently. The biggest obstacle is often the ego, which can drive individuals to seek recognition and assert dominance. In a society that frequently rewards self-promotion and competitiveness, practicing humility can sometimes feel countercultural.

Moreover, humility is sometimes mistaken for meekness or a lack of ambition. However, true humility is compatible with strong leadership and a healthy drive for achievement. It is about pursuing one's goals with respect for others and without arrogance or entitlement.

Cultivating Humility

Cultivating humility requires intentional practice. One effective method is mindfulness, which involves being present and fully engaged in the current moment without judgment. Mindfulness helps individuals recognize their thoughts and feelings about themselves and others, providing an opportunity to adjust attitudes toward greater humility.

Engaging in service-oriented activities can also foster humility. Volunteering for community service, for instance, can provide perspective on one's own life and challenges, highlighting the struggles and hardships others face. This can reduce egocentric behavior and increase empathy, encouraging a more humble approach to life.

Reflecting on the vastness of the universe and the transitory nature of life can also promote humility. Such reflection can help individuals realize the limited scope of their existence and the interconnectedness of all life, which naturally leads to a humbler outlook.

Living with Humility

Living with humility enriches one's life and the lives of those around them. It enhances personal freedom, as humble individuals are not chained by the desires for approval and recognition. They experience greater satisfaction in their achievements and relationships, secure in the knowledge that they are living authentically and respectfully.

Humility is a quiet yet powerful strength that promotes personal growth, enhances relationships, and fosters a compassionate community. It requires conscious effort to develop and maintain but results in a more balanced, fulfilling, and ethical way of living. Through humility, individuals can achieve a deeper sense of peace and a clearer perspective on what truly matters in life.

ϸϸϸ

"Humility is the quiet warrior of the spiritual
virtues; it does not shout but softly guides our
actions. It teaches us that true greatness lies in
being of service to others."

ᗷᗷᗷ

SIX

GRATITUDE: APPRECIATING LIFE'S GIFTS

Gratitude is a profound and enriching attitude that has been universally recognized across various cultures and spiritual traditions as essential for full and joyful living. It is more than merely saying thanks; it involves a deep appreciation for the people, experiences, and tangible gifts we receive daily. This sense of thankfulness can significantly enhance one's emotional and psychological resilience, contributing to greater happiness and a more fulfilled life.

The Psychological and Spiritual Benefits of Gratitude

At its core, gratitude is known to foster both psychological well-being and spiritual growth. Psychologically, practicing gratitude consistently has been linked to a host of benefits, including increased levels of happiness, reduced depression, and greater satisfaction with life. People who actively count their blessings tend to be happier and less depressed. This positive mental health outcome is likely because gratitude helps individuals focus on what they have rather than what they lack, which shifts their perception towards abundance rather than scarcity.

Spiritually, gratitude is often seen as a gateway to higher consciousness and deeper connection to the divine, whatever one's personal understanding of that might be. In many spiritual practices, gratitude is the heart's response to life's infinite blessings, which enhances one's connection with the universe. This connection encourages a type of humility and acceptance that is foundational for spiritual depth and maturity.

Cultivating a Habit of Gratitude

Developing a habit of gratitude involves more than occasional moments of thankfulness. It requires a consistent practice that can be cultivated through various means. One effective practice is keeping a gratitude journal. Regularly writing down things for which one is thankful can significantly increase awareness of life's positives and decrease the natural human tendency to focus on negatives. This practice can shift one's mindset from one of deficit and dissatisfaction to one of appreciation and profound contentment.

Another method is gratitude meditation or prayer, which involves reflecting on the day's events and acknowledging the good in them. This could be as simple as being thankful for the warmth of the sun, the comfort of a home, or the smile from a stranger. By meditating on these gifts, individuals can deepen their sense of gratitude and enhance their overall spiritual practice.

Gratitude in Relationships

Expressing gratitude within personal relationships can transform and deepen connections. When people express genuine appreciation for each other, it builds trust and mutual respect.

Acknowledging the positive aspects of relationships and vocalizing thankfulness for the partner's actions can alleviate conflicts and increase the resilience of the relationship. This is particularly true in long-term relationships, where the daily expression of gratitude can prevent the taking for granted of loved ones.

Moreover, gratitude can play a critical role in broader social interactions. In the workplace, for example, a culture of gratitude can lead to greater employee satisfaction and loyalty. Managers who regularly express gratitude to their teams can foster a more cooperative and cheerful work environment. Similarly, friends who consistently acknowledge and appreciate each other's qualities and efforts tend to maintain stronger, more enduring friendships.

Gratitude During Challenges

One of the more profound aspects of gratitude is its power to transform difficult situations. When faced with challenges, maintaining a perspective of gratitude can help individuals find meaning and value in their trials, which often leads to greater personal growth. This doesn't mean ignoring pain or glossing over problems but rather finding a silver lining among the difficulties. For instance, the challenges of a job loss can be mitigated by being grateful for the opportunity to reassess one's career path or to spend more time with family.

Furthermore, gratitude can be a powerful tool for resilience in the face of life's adversities. By focusing on what is still good when faced with significant losses—such as health, relationships, or material stability—individuals can navigate through their darkest times. This focus does not negate the pain or struggle but provides a lifeline during those challenging periods.

Living a Life of Gratitude

Ultimately, living a life of gratitude is about fostering an attitude of perpetual thankfulness for the myriad blessings, large and small, that life offers. This approach to life encourages a joyous and abundant mindset, which can influence all areas of life, including one's mental health, relationships, and spiritual growth. Grateful people often find themselves more deeply connected to others, more peaceful in their own skins, and more satisfied with their lives.

Gratitude is not just an emotional response but a deeper recognition of the abundance of life's blessings. It is an essential component of a well-lived and joyful life, cultivating an atmosphere of contentment, connection, and overall well-being. By integrating gratitude into daily practice, individuals not only enrich their own lives but also contribute to a more compassionate and appreciative world.

ppp

"Gratitude turns what we have into enough, and
more. It bridges the gap between scarcity and
abundance, teaching us that true richness is found
in appreciating the present."

ppp

SEVEN

PATIENCE: EMBRACING LIFE'S PACE

Patience is a virtue often celebrated in spiritual and philosophical traditions but challenging to cultivate in the fast-paced modern world. It involves the ability to tolerate delay, frustration, or suffering without becoming agitated or upset. Patience is more than just waiting; it's an active engagement in the present moment, recognizing and accepting the natural flow of life. Embracing patience can lead to a more contented life, reducing stress and improving relationships.

Understanding the Nature of Patience

Patience is fundamentally about self-control. It requires an individual to hold back immediate reactions and consider the long-term effects of their actions. This can mean waiting for the right moment to act, enduring a difficult situation without complaint, or continuing to work toward a goal when results are not immediately visible. Patience is connected to perseverance and resilience, as it often demands a steady commitment to a goal despite obstacles.

The spiritual significance of patience is profound. Many spiritual traditions view patience as essential to understanding life's deeper truths. It allows individuals to transcend their immediate desires and connect with a more enduring order of existence. In this view, patience is not passive waiting but an active discipline that refines the spirit and deepens understanding.

The Benefits of Patience

Practicing patience has numerous psychological benefits. It can lower stress levels, reduce feelings of anger and frustration, and lead to better decision-making. Patient individuals tend to experience less depression and anxiety and have better overall mental health. This is likely because patience helps to moderate the pressure of immediate expectations, allowing for a more measured and mindful approach to life's challenges.

Patience also enhances relationships. It allows for better communication because it gives individuals the time to consider their words carefully and to listen more attentively to others. In conflicts, patience can help de-escalate tension and foster a resolution that is acceptable to all parties. It helps build long-lasting relationships based on respect and understanding, rather than impulsive reactions.

Cultivating Patience in Everyday Life

Developing patience requires practice and mindfulness. One effective method is through meditation, which trains the mind to focus on the present moment and reduce the rush of compulsive thoughts and actions. Regular meditation can help cultivate a state of calmness that supports patient behavior.

Another way to develop patience is by setting realistic expectations.

Often, impatience stems from a mismatch between our expectations and reality. By setting more achievable goals and recognizing that some things take time, it's possible to reduce feelings of frustration and impatience.

Recognizing triggers that cause impatience is also crucial. This can involve tracking when you feel most impatient and understanding the reasons behind these feelings. Such awareness can help you anticipate and manage situations that might test your patience.

Patience as a Social Virtue

Patience is not just an individual virtue but a social one, promoting greater harmony and understanding in communities. In a society, patience can help smooth interactions in a world of diverse opinions and backgrounds. It encourages dialogue and cooperation, reducing conflicts and misunderstandings.

In the workplace, patience contributes to a positive environment where individuals feel valued and heard. It can improve team dynamics and productivity, as people are more likely to collaborate effectively when they feel that their pace and style of working are respected.

Challenges in Practicing Patience

Despite its benefits, patience can be challenging to practice consistently. Modern culture often emphasizes speed and immediate results, which can make patience seem like an obstacle rather than a virtue. Furthermore, everyday stressors and pressures can erode our capacity for patience, making it easier to succumb to irritability or anger.

Overcoming these challenges requires a conscious commitment to developing patience as a habit. It involves recognizing the value of waiting and seeing the benefits that patience can bring to one's mental health and relationships.

Living with Patience

Living with patience means embracing life's pace and its inherent delays and difficulties. It involves understanding that not all things happen as quickly as one might like and that real growth and understanding come from the ability to wait and persevere through challenges.

Patience is a profound virtue that offers numerous benefits. It enriches personal life by enhancing mental health and strengthening relationships. Socially, it fosters a more harmonious community. Cultivating patience allows individuals to live more peaceful, fulfilled lives, embracing the natural pace of life with grace and resilience.

ﭠﭠﭠ

"Patience is not simply waiting; it is maintaining grace in the face of adversity. It teaches us that all things unfold in their own time."

EIGHT

MINDFULNESS: LIVING IN THE MOMENT

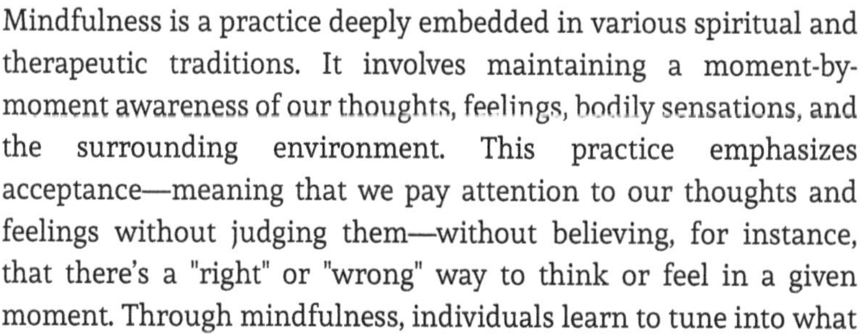

Mindfulness is a practice deeply embedded in various spiritual and therapeutic traditions. It involves maintaining a moment-by-moment awareness of our thoughts, feelings, bodily sensations, and the surrounding environment. This practice emphasizes acceptance—meaning that we pay attention to our thoughts and feelings without judging them—without believing, for instance, that there's a "right" or "wrong" way to think or feel in a given moment. Through mindfulness, individuals learn to tune into what they are sensing in the present moment rather than rehashing the past or imagining the future.

The Essence of Mindfulness

At its core, mindfulness is about presence. It is the act of bringing one's attention to the experiences occurring in the present moment. This can be practiced through meditation, but it is also about being conscious and attentive in daily life. Mindfulness is the opposite of mindlessness—it involves being conscious of life as it happens and not being caught up in automatic or habitual reactions. This presence of mind provides a greater capacity to cope with everyday events and greater engagement with life and its challenges.

Practicing mindfulness involves observing bodily sensations, thoughts, and emotions from moment to moment. By cultivating this awareness, individuals can better recognize their usual patterns of mind, which can dominate their life. This realization can empower individuals to change these patterns and respond to life's challenges in new, more effective ways.

Benefits of Mindfulness

The practice of mindfulness has numerous benefits that enhance both mental and physical well-being. Psychologically, it reduces stress, anxiety, and depression. Mindfulness helps break the chain of everyday thought patterns that can lead to these states. For example, by noticing the warning signs of stress early, one can take steps to manage stressors more effectively.

Physiologically, mindfulness practices have been found to improve health outcomes as varied as lowering blood pressure, reducing chronic pain, and improving sleep. These benefits arise because mindfulness reduces the body's stress responses, which can exacerbate many health issues. Moreover, it enhances resilience and the ability to hold pain and distress more comfortably.

Mindfulness and Relationships

Practicing mindfulness can significantly improve interpersonal relationships. By being fully present with others, one can engage more deeply and listen more intently. This enhances communication and empathy within relationships, making conflicts easier to resolve and mutual understandings more accessible to achieve. Mindfulness allows individuals to respond to situations with calmness and insight, rather than reacting impulsively.

Moreover, mindfulness cultivates a greater capacity for compassion and empathy. It encourages an openness and acceptance of others which fosters deeper bonds and more satisfying relationships. By reducing reactive behavior, mindfulness supports more balanced and harmonious interactions with others.

Cultivating Mindfulness in Daily Life

Integrating mindfulness into everyday life is both a challenge and an opportunity. It starts with simple practices such as mindful breathing, where focus is placed on the breath, noticing each inhale and exhale. This can serve as a foundation for extending mindfulness to other activities.

Eating, walking, and listening are other activities that can be done mindfully by fully engaging with the sensory experiences they offer. For instance, mindful eating involves paying attention to the taste, texture, and aroma of food, which can lead to greater satisfaction with meals and can aid digestion and portion control.

Setting aside time for formal mindfulness meditation is also beneficial. This might include daily sessions of mindfulness practices such as body scans, seated meditation, or yoga. These practices help develop the ability to bring mindful awareness more naturally and effectively into everyday life.

Challenges in Practicing Mindfulness

Despite its many benefits, practicing mindfulness can be challenging. It requires consistent practice and dedication. Many find it difficult to find time in their busy schedules to practice mindfulness regularly. Furthermore, becoming more aware of one's thoughts and feelings can sometimes be uncomfortable, as this can bring heightened awareness to underlying issues or stressors.

However, the rewards of consistent mindfulness practice can be profound. It offers a way to live more fully, engaging with the present in a meaningful and positive way.

Living with Mindfulness

Ultimately, living with mindfulness means embracing each moment with awareness and grace. It allows individuals to experience the richness of each day, reducing the regret of dwelling on the past or the anxiety of planning for the future. Mindfulness fosters a deep-seated peace by aligning individuals more closely with their authentic selves and their environment.

Mindfulness is a transformative practice that opens the door to a richer, more fulfilling life. It strengthens mental resilience, enhances physical health, and deepens relationships. Mindfulness teaches living in harmony with the complexities of life, embracing each moment with attention and care.

ppp

"Mindfulness invites us to live deeply, in each
moment, free from the distractions of past regrets
and future anxieties. It is the art of being wholly
present, where life truly unfolds."

ᗷᗷᗷ

NINE

GENEROSITY: THE JOY OF GIVING

Generosity is a virtue that transcends cultures, religions, and societies, often regarded as one of the key components to living a fulfilling and meaningful life. It involves giving freely and selflessly to others, whether through sharing time, resources, or talents. The act of giving can generate profound joy and satisfaction, not only for the recipient but also for the giver. This virtue encompasses more than just charitable donations; it is a broader attitude of kindness and a willingness to support others.

Understanding the Essence of Generosity

Generosity is fundamentally about selflessness and the desire to improve the well-being of others. It's an empathetic impulse that acknowledges the needs and hardships of others and responds with heartfelt actions. Generous individuals often find themselves more connected to the community and to humanity as a whole, as generosity helps to bridge differences and foster a sense of solidarity among people.

The practice of generosity involves a conscious decision to give without expecting anything in return. This can manifest in various forms—from volunteering at a local food bank to offering emotional support to a friend. The scope of generosity is not confined by the material aspect; it also includes the generosity of spirit, such as offering kindness, attention, and respect.

Psychological and Social Benefits of Generosity

Engaging in acts of generosity has been shown to provide substantial psychological benefits. Research indicates that giving can boost the giver's mood, leading to a phenomenon often referred to as the "helper's high." This is believed to be due to the release of endorphins, which are natural mood lifters. Additionally, being generous can decrease stress and contribute to a longer, healthier life.

From a social perspective, generosity strengthens communities by fostering trust and cooperation. It plays a critical role in building and maintaining social bonds, as generous acts are often reciprocated, creating a cycle of giving that strengthens group ties. This reciprocity is not just about direct payback but also about nurturing a culture of care and support within the community.

Cultivating a Generous Spirit

Developing a habit of generosity involves both mindset and action. Cultivating an attitude of abundance is key—seeing life as full of opportunities to give and understanding that sharing one's resources does not lead to deprivation but rather enriches one's life. Recognizing that generosity leads to greater happiness and connectedness can motivate individuals to incorporate more giving into their daily lives.

Mindfulness and gratitude also play crucial roles in fostering generosity. Being mindful allows individuals to notice the needs of others, while gratitude fills them with an appreciation of their own resources, which often motivates sharing. These mindful and grateful attitudes can transform generosity from an occasional act to a daily practice.

Challenges to Practicing Generosity

While the benefits of generosity are significant, there are also challenges that can inhibit generous behavior. In some cases, individuals may feel they do not have enough resources or time to give to others. Economic strain, personal responsibilities, or simply a perceived lack of surplus can restrain one's willingness or ability to be generous.

Furthermore, there can be cultural or societal barriers to generosity. In highly competitive environments, for instance, giving may be seen as a weakness or a futile expenditure. Overcoming these challenges requires a shift in perspective, recognizing that generosity enriches both giver and receiver, and that it can be practiced in many ways, not all of which require significant resources.

Generosity in Practice

To integrate generosity more fully into one's life, it can be helpful to start small and simple. Regular acts of kindness, like paying for a stranger's coffee or offering a compliment, can set the foundation for more substantial acts of giving. Planning for generosity, such as setting aside time each week to help others or budgeting for charitable donations, can also make giving a regular part of life.

Sharing one's skills and knowledge is another form of generosity that can have a profound impact. Whether it's mentoring a young professional or teaching a skill to someone, these acts of generosity can leverage personal strengths for the benefit of others.

Living Generously

Embracing a lifestyle of generosity involves viewing every interaction and every day as an opportunity to give. Those who live generously often find that their lives are richer and more meaningful. They experience deeper relationships, a greater sense of community, and an enhanced sense of personal satisfaction.

Generosity is not just an act but a way of living that celebrates the joy of giving and the deep connections it fosters. It is a powerful pathway to personal growth and social harmony, offering benefits to both the giver and the receiver. By adopting a generous mindset, individuals can transform their lives and the lives of those around them, spreading joy and kindness in a world that greatly needs it.

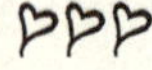

"Generosity is the pure joy of giving without the
expectation of receiving. It is understanding that
the true measure of our lives is how much we give of
ourselves."

ᑭᑭᑭ

TEN

COURAGE: FACING FEARS WITH FAITH

Courage is not the absence of fear, but the triumph over it. It's a vital attribute for anyone looking to live a meaningful, purpose-driven life. This profound quality allows individuals to confront fears, uncertainties, and challenges with fortitude and faith. In a broader sense, courage is about persisting in the face of adversity and choosing to act in alignment with one's values and beliefs, even when it's difficult or risky to do so.

The Essence of Courage

Courage involves both physical bravery and moral strength. It can manifest as the ability to stand up for what is right, to speak out against injustice, or to undertake actions that are fraught with personal risks. Courage is deeply interwoven with integrity, as it often requires adherence to moral convictions that are tested in challenging circumstances. This could mean anything from a firefighter running into a burning building to save lives, to an individual standing up against social injustices, or someone admitting their mistakes openly, despite potential repercussions.

In the spiritual realm, courage often involves facing the internal battles of doubt and fear with a steadfast faith in a higher power or deeper purpose. This kind of spiritual courage empowers individuals to overcome obstacles that might otherwise seem insurmountable, reinforcing their faith and spiritual growth.

Benefits of Cultivating Courage

The cultivation of courage has numerous benefits. It enhances self-confidence and promotes resilience, allowing individuals to recover quickly from setbacks. Courageous actions lead to personal growth and often result in a broader perspective on life's challenges, helping individuals to not only navigate difficult situations but also to emerge stronger and more adept.

Moreover, courage can lead to increased satisfaction in life. By facing fears and not allowing them to dictate actions, individuals open themselves to new experiences, opportunities, and the true fulfillment of their potential. Courage also fosters respect and admiration from others, which can enhance interpersonal relationships and open up leadership opportunities.

Cultivating Courage in Everyday Life

Developing courage is a gradual process that involves expanding one's comfort zones and confronting fears systematically. One effective approach is to start with small challenges that stretch personal limits but are manageable. Successfully navigating these smaller challenges builds the confidence and momentum needed to tackle larger issues.

Reflection is also a crucial tool in cultivating courage. Understanding what one fears, and why, can demystify fears and diminish their power. Journaling, meditation, and dialogues with trusted friends or mentors can aid in this reflective process, offering insights and reinforcement.

Another key element is the reinforcement of a positive mindset. Affirmations and visualization techniques can help solidify the belief in one's ability to act courageously. Visualizing oneself successfully facing a fear can mentally and emotionally prepare an individual to do it in real life.

Courage in the Face of Adversity

Courage is particularly important when facing significant life adversities such as illness, loss, or major life changes. In these moments, courage helps individuals to confront painful realities with hope and determination. This might mean having the courage to seek help, to change unhealthy behaviors, or to let go of past hurts and move forward.

Spiritual faith often plays a crucial role in these situations, providing the strength and assurance that one is not alone in their struggles. Faith can anchor an individual, giving them the courage to endure and overcome the challenges they face.

Social Courage

Courage also has a vital social dimension. It empowers individuals to stand up for others, challenge unfair practices, and participate in movements for social change. This type of courage is crucial for creating a just society where all individuals can thrive. It involves advocating for vulnerable or marginalized communities and striving to uphold ethical standards in all areas of life.

Living a Courageous Life

Embracing a courageous lifestyle means being ready to face every day with determination and optimism, regardless of what it might bring. It requires a continuous commitment to live by one's principles, even when it's inconvenient or frightening. Such a lifestyle not only enriches one's own life but also inspires and uplifts those around them.

Courage is a transformative quality that changes how individuals view and interact with the world. It is essential for both personal growth and social development. By facing fears with courage and faith, individuals can lead more fulfilling lives and contribute to a more courageous and resilient society. This quality, while challenging to cultivate, offers profound rewards, enabling people to live authentically and with integrity in the face of life's many challenges.

 PPP

"Courage is not the absence of fear but the triumph over it. It is the brave heart that faces the storm and dares to sail into uncharted waters."

❦❦❦

ELEVEN

SERENITY: FINDING CALM IN THE CHAOS

Serenity is a state of being calm, peaceful, and untroubled, emerging as a beacon for those navigating the stormy waters of modern life. It is a quality that has been sought after by philosophers, poets, and spiritual leaders alike. In a world that seems increasingly dominated by chaos and noise, finding serenity is more relevant and necessary than ever. This tranquility of mind is not merely an escape from life's challenges but a profound way to engage with them more constructively and peacefully.

Understanding Serenity

Serenity involves more than just the absence of stress or anxiety; it encompasses a deep sense of peace and contentment that comes from within. This inner peace allows individuals to maintain calm and clarity in the face of adversity, making wise decisions and handling difficulties with grace. The serene mind is resilient, possessing the quiet strength to weather life's storms without being overwhelmed.

At its core, serenity is closely linked to acceptance. This acceptance is not about resignation or passivity but about recognizing and embracing the reality of the present moment. By accepting things as they are, one can avoid the turmoil that comes from resisting reality and can find peace even in difficult circumstances.

Cultivating Serenity through Mindfulness and Meditation

One of the most effective ways to cultivate serenity is through mindfulness and meditation. These practices focus on bringing one's attention fully to the present moment and observing what occurs without judgment. By regularly practicing mindfulness, individuals can decrease their usual reactions to stress and develop a more peaceful state of mind.

Meditation, particularly practices that emphasize stillness and the observation of thoughts, can significantly enhance one's capacity for serenity. These quiet moments allow the mind to settle and reduce the internal noise that often leads to anxiety and stress. Over time, the practice of meditation can lead to profound shifts in how one experiences the world, fostering a deeper sense of calm and peace.

The Role of Nature in Serenity

Engaging with the natural world is another powerful way to achieve serenity. Nature's inherent beauty and rhythm can have a calming effect on the mind and spirit. Activities like walking in a forest, sitting by a lake, or simply spending time in a garden can help reduce stress levels and promote feelings of peace.

Moreover, nature provides a reminder of the natural cycles of life, encouraging acceptance of the ebb and flow of existence. This perspective can help reduce the anxiety that comes from trying to control the uncontrollable, allowing for a more serene engagement with life's complexities.

Serenity in Relationships

Serenity can also transform one's personal relationships. A serene individual often radiates a calming presence that can soothe and uplift others. By maintaining a peaceful center, one can approach conflicts and challenges in relationships with a clear, calm mind, facilitating better communication and understanding.

Furthermore, serenity allows for deeper connections with others because it fosters a non-reactive, listening presence. This can enhance empathy and compassion, both crucial for healthy and supportive relationships.

Challenges to Maintaining Serenity

Achieving and maintaining serenity is not without its challenges. The chaos of daily life, personal responsibilities, and global crises can all disrupt a serene state of mind. Moreover, the cultural emphasis on busyness and productivity often means that taking time to cultivate serenity is seen as a luxury rather than a necessity.

To overcome these challenges, it is helpful to integrate practices that foster serenity into daily life. This might involve setting aside time for quiet reflection, practicing breathing exercises during stressful situations, or establishing regular routines that include activities promoting peace and calm.

Living with Serenity

Living a life characterized by serenity does not mean avoiding challenges or always feeling peaceful. Instead, it means approaching life's complexities with a calm, steady presence that enables one to face whatever comes with equanimity and grace. This approach can lead to a more joyful, impactful, and harmonious existence.

Serenity is a profound quality that can greatly enhance one's life, offering a peaceful refuge in the midst of chaos. By cultivating serenity through mindfulness, connection with nature, and other supportive practices, individuals can not only improve their own lives but also bring peace and understanding to their interactions with others. Embracing serenity allows for a life lived with depth, purpose, and calm, no matter the external circumstances.

ϷϷϷ

"Serenity is not found in the absence of chaos but in the calm within it. It is the stillness that remains when the storm has passed."

ᛒᛒᛒ

TWELVE

WISDOM: LEARNING FROM LIFE'S LESSONS

Wisdom is often considered one of the most esteemed virtues, a culmination of knowledge, experience, and deep understanding that guides one through life's complexities with discernment and insight. It is more than just intelligence or the accumulation of factual knowledge; it involves the thoughtful integration of experience into a coherent understanding of people, events, and situations. Wisdom allows individuals to navigate life's challenges with clarity and make decisions that are informed not only by facts but also by compassion and ethical considerations.

The Nature of Wisdom

Wisdom is typically seen as developing from a combination of diverse life experiences, the ability to learn from those experiences, and the reflection on those lessons. It involves a balanced approach to emotions and reasoning, resulting in deep, meaningful insights into the human condition and the nature of the world. Wisdom is not static; it grows and evolves over time, deepened by ongoing experiences and continuous learning.

One of the core components of wisdom is emotional regulation—the ability to manage one's emotions, understand others' emotions, and navigate interpersonal dynamics effectively. This emotional intelligence is crucial for making prudent decisions that are not only logically sound but also morally considerate and empathetic.

Wisdom in Decision-Making

In decision-making, wisdom involves considering various perspectives and potential outcomes, looking beyond immediate or easy solutions, and thinking long-term. Wise individuals are known for their ability to see the bigger picture and avoid making decisions based purely on emotion or self-interest. This often means considering what is best for others and the greater good, even at a personal cost.

Wisdom also includes a keen sense of timing, knowing when to act and when to wait, which can be crucial in both personal and professional contexts. This aspect of wisdom prevents rash decisions and promotes actions that are thoughtful and well-considered.

Cultivating Wisdom through Reflection and Openness

Wisdom is cultivated through deliberate reflection on past experiences and the conscious integration of those reflections into one's life and behavior. Keeping a journal, engaging in thoughtful discussions, and meditating can all be effective ways to enhance self-reflection and promote wisdom.

Openness to new experiences and ideas is equally important. By exposing oneself to diverse situations and viewpoints, one can learn from a broader range of experiences, which can deepen understanding and enhance wisdom. This openness involves humility and the recognition that no one person can ever know everything, and that there is always room for growth.

Wisdom and Relationships

Wisdom plays a critical role in relationships. It enables individuals to communicate more effectively, understand deeper emotional undercurrents, and respond to others with empathy and tact. Wise individuals can often help resolve conflicts by finding common ground and fostering mutual understanding.

Furthermore, wisdom involves an appreciation of life's complexity, including the recognition that people are multifaceted and that life events often have multiple, interlocking causes and effects. This understanding can lead to more compassionate and supportive relationships.

Challenges in Developing Wisdom

The path to wisdom is not without its challenges. It often involves difficult experiences and the emotional pain of mistakes. However, these difficulties are also what propel growth and learning. The key is not to avoid these challenges but to engage with them constructively, using them as opportunities to develop deeper insight and understanding.

In a culture that often prioritizes immediate gratification and superficial achievements, cultivating wisdom can sometimes seem counterintuitive. It requires patience, persistence, and a commitment to personal growth that goes beyond the superficial.

The Impact of Wisdom on Personal and Professional Life

In professional settings, wisdom is invaluable for leadership. It promotes fair and moral management, enhances problem-solving skills, and improves team dynamics. Leaders who exhibit wisdom are often respected and admired for their thoughtful, inclusive approach to management and their ability to inspire and guide their teams through challenges.

In personal life, wisdom enriches one's experiences and relationships. It provides a framework for understanding life's ups and downs and integrating these experiences into a coherent, meaningful life narrative. This can lead to a greater sense of peace and fulfillment.

Living Wisely

Ultimately, living wisely means embracing life's uncertainties and complexities with openness and curiosity. It involves continuously learning from experiences, reflecting on those lessons, and applying them in various aspects of life. By valuing wisdom, individuals can lead richer, more thoughtful lives that not only benefit themselves but also contribute to the well-being of others around them.

Wisdom is a profound virtue that enhances life's quality and depth. It allows individuals to navigate the world with insight, empathy, and moral clarity, making decisions that are not only good for themselves but also for their communities and the broader world. Wisdom is not simply about knowing what to do but understanding why, a critical aspect of living a truly enriched life.

ᐁᐁᐁ

"Wisdom is the light that illuminates our path
through the complexities of life. It is gained through
experience, tempered by reflection, and shared
through actions."

ʬʬʬ

THIRTEEN

EMPATHY: WALKING IN ANOTHER'S SHOES

Empathy, the capacity to understand and share the feelings of others, is a cornerstone of human social interaction. It allows individuals to navigate the complexities of interpersonal relationships, enhances communication, and fosters a sense of community and understanding. Empathy goes beyond mere sympathy, which is feeling compassion or sorrow for the hardships of others; it involves a deeper connection, where one experiences the emotions of another person as if they were their own.

Understanding Empathy

Empathy involves several components, including the emotional aspect, where one literally feels what another person is feeling, and the cognitive aspect, which is the ability to understand another person's point of view and emotions intellectually. These components work together to help individuals connect with others on a profound level, promoting better communication and stronger relationships.

Empathy is not an innate talent but a skill that can be developed and enhanced over time. It requires an openness to the experiences of others, as well as a willingness to engage with and understand those experiences. This development is crucial for personal relationships, effective leadership, and maintaining social harmony.

The Benefits of Empathy

The benefits of cultivating empathy are extensive. On a personal level, empathy enriches relationships, making them more satisfying and stable. Empathetic individuals are often more attuned to the needs and feelings of their partners, friends, and family, which can lead to more fulfilling interactions and a deeper sense of connection.

In professional settings, empathy is invaluable in leadership and teamwork. Leaders who show empathy towards their employees often inspire greater loyalty and higher morale, and teams with empathetic members tend to experience better collaboration and less conflict. Empathy can also enhance customer service by enabling workers to understand and meet the needs of clients more effectively.

Empathy and Conflict Resolution

Empathy plays a critical role in conflict resolution. By understanding and validating the emotions and perspectives of all parties involved, empathetic individuals can help de-escalate tensions and facilitate a solution that is acceptable to everyone. This capacity to mediate and negotiate is especially important in multicultural settings, where differing values and expectations can lead to misunderstandings.

Moreover, empathy contributes to social cohesion by fostering an environment where individuals feel understood and valued. This is particularly important in diverse societies, where empathy can bridge cultural and social gaps and promote mutual respect.

Cultivating Empathy

Developing empathy involves several practices that encourage a greater understanding of others. Active listening is one of the most important—paying close attention to what others are saying, both verbally and nonverbally, without immediately forming a response or judgment. This practice helps individuals gain a deeper appreciation of others' perspectives and emotions.

Reading extensively and engaging with diverse media can also enhance empathy. Literature, films, and other forms of storytelling provide insights into the lives and experiences of others, often different from one's own, which can broaden one's emotional and intellectual horizons.

Practicing mindfulness can further develop empathy. By becoming more aware of one's own thoughts and feelings, it becomes easier to recognize and understand the emotions of others. Mindfulness practices help cultivate a presence that is open and receptive to the feelings and experiences of others.

Challenges to Empathy

Despite its importance, empathy faces several challenges in modern society. The fast pace of life and the often superficial nature of digital communication can inhibit deep, empathetic connections. Furthermore, societal divisions—whether political, cultural, or economic—can foster an environment of suspicion and division that makes empathy more difficult.

Overcoming these challenges requires intentional effort.

Individuals and communities must prioritize empathy, taking steps to cultivate understanding and connection actively. This might involve community programs, educational curricula focusing on empathy, or workplace training that encourages empathetic leadership and cooperation.

Empathy in Action

Empathy must be more than a passive emotion; it requires active expression. This can take many forms, from providing emotional support to someone in distress to engaging in charitable work that seeks to alleviate the suffering of others. On a larger scale, empathy can drive social and political changes by highlighting issues of injustice and promoting a more inclusive society.

Empathy is not just a valuable interpersonal skill but a fundamental component of a functioning society. It enriches personal relationships, enhances professional environments, and plays a crucial role in conflict resolution and social cohesion. By actively cultivating empathy, individuals can contribute to a more understanding and compassionate world. This practice not only benefits others but also enriches one's own life, creating deeper connections and a greater sense of purpose and fulfillment.

$$\triangleright\triangleright\triangleright$$

"Empathy is the bridge that connects disparate souls, allowing us to feel with others, not just for them. It teaches us that love is a language that transcends words."

❤❤❤

FOURTEEN

JUSTICE: ADVOCATING FOR FAIRNESS

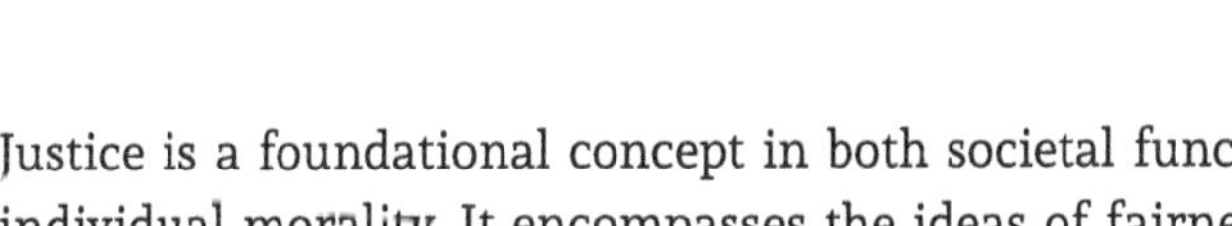

Justice is a foundational concept in both societal functioning and individual morality. It encompasses the ideas of fairness, equality, and the right treatment of individuals, underpinned by the principle that all individuals deserve to be treated with respect and dignity. Advocating for justice involves striving towards a balance where everyone has equal opportunities and is held to the same standards, regardless of their background, status, or personal characteristics.

The Essence of Justice

Justice is multi-faceted, involving various types such as distributive justice, which concerns the fair allocation of resources; procedural justice, focusing on fairness in the processes that resolve disputes and allocate resources; and restorative justice, which seeks to heal and restore relationships after wrongdoing. These forms of justice are not mutually exclusive but are interrelated, each contributing to the comprehensive understanding and implementation of justice in society.

At its core, justice is about ensuring that every individual receives what they are due, whether in terms of rights, resources, or recognition. This requires an understanding of the complexities of human needs and the societal structures that impact how those needs are met.

Justice in Society

In societal terms, justice plays a crucial role in maintaining order and harmony. It is the cornerstone of lawful and civil conduct, providing a framework within which individuals can coexist peacefully. Laws and regulations, ideally, are crafted to uphold justice by protecting individuals' rights and ensuring fair treatment for all.

However, the challenge in any society is the effective implementation of these laws in a way that truly reflects the principle of justice. This involves ongoing efforts to refine legal systems according to evolving understandings of what fairness means and how it should be achieved. Advocating for justice often requires vigilance and activism to challenge unjust laws and practices and to champion reforms that enhance fairness and equality.

The Role of Individuals in Promoting Justice

Individuals play a critical role in advocating for justice. This can involve participation in democratic processes, such as voting, campaigning for political candidates who prioritize justice, or directly engaging in legislative processes through petitions or lobbying. Individuals can also join or support organizations that work towards judicial reforms or equality for underrepresented or disadvantaged groups.

On a more personal level, advocating for justice can mean standing up against injustices in everyday life—whether by confronting discriminatory behaviors, supporting victims of injustice, or spreading awareness about justice issues through education and dialogue. Each of these actions contributes to a broader culture of fairness and respect for rights.

Educational Initiatives in Promoting Justice

Education is a powerful tool in promoting justice. Educational programs that focus on civic education, human rights, and ethical reasoning can equip individuals with the knowledge and skills they need to understand justice issues and engage in advocacy. Schools and universities play pivotal roles in shaping the perspectives of young individuals on justice, fairness, and equality.

Moreover, education that promotes critical thinking and empathy can encourage individuals to look beyond their personal experiences and understand the broader social implications of justice. This kind of education fosters a more informed and engaged citizenry capable of contributing to a more just society.

Challenges in the Pursuit of Justice

Advocating for justice is fraught with challenges. These include resistance from those who benefit from the status quo, the complexity of changing entrenched societal structures, and the often slow pace of legal and cultural change. Moreover, notions of what is 'just' can vary greatly between different cultures and communities, complicating efforts to define and implement fair practices universally.

Another significant challenge is the potential for burnout among those who fight for justice. The emotional toll of confronting injustice, especially when progress is slow and setbacks are frequent, can be substantial. Support networks, self-care practices, and maintaining a balance between activism and personal life are essential for sustainability in justice advocacy.

Justice as a Way of Life

Ultimately, justice is more than just a set of principles or legal guidelines—it is a way of life. It involves continuously striving to live in a way that respects and upholds the dignity of all individuals. This includes being informed, aware, and active in one's community and society at large.

Justice is an essential part of creating a society where all individuals can thrive. Advocating for justice requires a multifaceted approach that includes legal action, education, personal commitment, and societal engagement. By actively participating in these efforts, individuals can help build a world that is fairer and more equitable for everyone. This journey is complex and challenging but is undoubtedly one of the most crucial undertakings in any society.

ppp

"Justice is the cornerstone of a society that values each individual equally. It demands vigilance and courage, for it is not simply inherited, but actively shaped in the choices we make every day."

ᏢᏢᏢ

FIFTEEN

Resilience: Spiritual Strength in Adversity

Resilience is the capacity to recover quickly from difficulties; it's a form of mental and spiritual toughness that enables individuals to navigate through adversity and emerge stronger. In the context of spiritual life, resilience is not just about bouncing back from challenges, but also about growing through them, often gaining deeper insights and a strengthened spirit. This spiritual resilience can be seen as a transformative process that deepens one's faith, broadens understanding, and reinforces commitment to one's values and beliefs.

Understanding Spiritual Resilience

Spiritual resilience is the ability to sustain one's spirit, soul, and sense of purpose in the face of life's challenges. It involves drawing on spiritual beliefs and practices to find meaning and strength during tough times. For many, this means connecting with a higher power, whether through prayer, meditation, or scripture reading. For others, it might involve a more personal or secular approach, such as reflecting on personal values or finding solace in nature and art.

The essence of spiritual resilience lies in the understanding that adversity is part of life's journey and that enduring hardship can lead to valuable life lessons and personal growth. This perspective helps individuals not just to survive tough times but to thrive during and after them.

Cultivating Spiritual Resilience

Building spiritual resilience is a proactive process that involves several key practices. One of the most effective is the development of a regular spiritual or reflective practice, such as meditation, prayer, or journaling. These practices help individuals maintain a connection to their inner selves and their values, providing a stable foundation when external circumstances are challenging.

Another important aspect of cultivating resilience is community. Being part of a supportive spiritual or social community provides emotional support, practical help, and a sense of belonging, all of which are crucial during difficult times. Community connections can offer encouragement and reminders of one's worth and potential, which might be obscured during periods of personal struggle.

Engaging with inspirational stories of others who have overcome adversity can also strengthen resilience. These stories can provide both comfort and a blueprint for navigating one's own challenges, highlighting the potential for recovery and growth.

The Role of Faith and Belief

Faith and belief are central to spiritual resilience. They provide a framework that helps individuals make sense of their suffering and maintain hope for the future. This might involve believing in a benevolent force that has a plan for them, the intrinsic value of each experience, or their own strength and capacity to overcome difficulties.

Beliefs can shape how adversity is interpreted and managed. For instance, viewing challenges as tests of faith or opportunities for growth can transform the emotional response to these situations, turning them from overwhelming obstacles into manageable elements of one's spiritual journey.

Adversity as an Opportunity for Growth

One of the key tenets of spiritual resilience is the concept of growth through adversity. Challenges are seen not just as barriers to happiness but as opportunities to enhance one's character, deepen understanding, and refine one's spirit. This growth is often manifested in increased empathy, heightened awareness, and a greater appreciation for life.

Spiritually resilient individuals often emerge from tough periods with a renewed sense of purpose and a clearer understanding of their priorities and values. This realignment can lead to significant life changes that bring more fulfillment and alignment with one's spiritual path.

Challenges in Developing Spiritual Resilience

While the benefits of spiritual resilience are significant, developing it is not without challenges. It requires a willingness to confront and process difficult emotions rather than avoiding them. This emotional work can be painful and demanding.

Additionally, in a culture that often prioritizes material success and external achievements, focusing on spiritual development can sometimes feel counter-cultural or undervalued. It can be challenging to maintain a commitment to spiritual growth in an environment that doesn't always support such endeavors.

Integrating Spiritual Resilience into Daily Life

To effectively integrate spiritual resilience into everyday life, individuals can practice mindfulness and gratitude, engage regularly with their spiritual community, and make time for reflection and meditation. They can also seek to embody the values they cherish, such as kindness, patience, and integrity, in their daily interactions and decisions.

Spiritual resilience is a profound source of strength and stability in the face of life's challenges. It involves a dynamic and continual process of building inner strength through spiritual practices, community support, and personal reflection. By developing spiritual resilience, individuals can navigate life's adversities with grace and emerge not only intact but enhanced, carrying forward lessons and insights that enrich their spiritual journey and overall well-being.

ᐅᐅᐅ

"Resilience is the inner flame that never
extinguishes; it shines brightest when the night is
darkest. It teaches us that the human spirit is
unbreakable, capable of overcoming any adversity."

ᚦᚦᚦ

SIXTEEN
PURITY: MAINTAINING SPIRITUAL CLARITY

Purity in a spiritual context is often interpreted as maintaining integrity and clarity in one's thoughts, actions, and interactions. It is not just about abstaining from physical impurities but encompasses a holistic approach to cleansing one's inner life. This includes fostering thoughts, emotions, and behaviors aligned with one's spiritual values and beliefs. Purity is thus seen as essential for deepening one's spiritual connection and living a more fulfilled and meaningful life.

Understanding Spiritual Purity

Spiritual purity involves a commitment to living according to the principles and values that one holds sacred. This can vary widely across different cultures and religious backgrounds, but common themes include honesty, compassion, self-discipline, and non-attachment. The practice of spiritual purity is about striving to embody these qualities in all aspects of life, from personal relationships to professional conduct.

At its core, spiritual purity is about the alignment of one's inner and outer worlds. It requires a conscious effort to filter out influences that might cloud one's spiritual vision or lead one away from their moral compass. This alignment helps individuals achieve a sense of peace and satisfaction, knowing that their lives reflect their deepest beliefs and aspirations.

Cultivating Spiritual Purity

The cultivation of spiritual purity typically involves both introspective and outward practices. Introspective practices include meditation, prayer, and reflective journaling, which help individuals gain insights into their thoughts and motivations and assess whether these are in harmony with their spiritual goals. Such practices provide the mental and emotional space necessary for recognizing and processing inner conflicts, desires, and attachments that may impede spiritual clarity.

Outward practices might involve engaging in acts of kindness, pursuing justice, and participating in community service. These activities can reinforce spiritual values and provide practical avenues for expressing and solidifying one's commitment to those values. Additionally, they often involve interaction with others who share similar values, which can strengthen one's resolve and provide mutual encouragement.

The Role of Discipline in Maintaining Purity

Discipline is a crucial aspect of maintaining spiritual purity. This includes the discipline to avoid situations or behaviors that conflict with one's spiritual values and the discipline to engage regularly in practices that enhance spiritual understanding and connection. For many, this might involve adhering to specific dietary laws, participating in religious observances, or maintaining a routine of prayer or meditation.

Discipline in this context is not about restriction but about freedom. It frees individuals from the distractions and impulses that cloud spiritual clarity and prevent them from living authentically in line with their beliefs.

Challenges to Spiritual Purity

Maintaining spiritual purity is not without its challenges. Modern life is rife with distractions, from the incessant pull of social media to the pressures of consumer culture, which can lead to a preoccupation with material wealth and status at the expense of spiritual values. Furthermore, the complexity of modern ethical dilemmas can sometimes make it difficult to discern the most spiritually aligned course of action.

Moreover, the journey towards spiritual purity often involves confronting uncomfortable truths about oneself, such as recognizing selfish or harmful tendencies. This level of self-scrutiny can be difficult and may require significant emotional resilience and courage.

Integrating Purity into Everyday Life

Integrating spiritual purity into daily life requires consistent effort and mindfulness. It involves regular self-examination and reflection to ensure that one's actions continue to align with their spiritual principles. It also may involve setting boundaries to protect one's spiritual practices from being undermined by less important activities or influences.

Education and community engagement are also important. Learning more about one's spiritual traditions can deepen understanding and commitment, while participating in a community can provide support and accountability. These interactions not only reinforce one's own practices but also offer opportunities to promote purity and positivity in the wider community.

Living with Spiritual Purity

Living a life that reflects spiritual purity brings numerous benefits, including deeper personal satisfaction, improved relationships, and a greater sense of peace and purpose. Those who successfully integrate this purity into their lives often find that they are better able to cope with life's challenges and are more resilient in the face of adversity.

Maintaining spiritual purity is a dynamic and ongoing process that involves continual growth and refinement. It requires diligence, discipline, and a commitment to living authentically according to one's spiritual beliefs. Those who undertake this journey often find it deeply rewarding, as it not only enhances personal well-being but also contributes to the cultivation of a more compassionate and understanding world.

ﭖﭖﭖ

"Purity in thought, word, and deed aligns us with our highest selves. It is the meticulous attention to the integrity of our daily actions that cultivates a life of harmony."

❦❦❦

SEVENTEEN

DEVOTION: DEEPENING YOUR SPIRITUAL COMMITMENT

Devotion is a profound dedication to a cause, an ideal, or a spiritual path. It involves a deep commitment that transcends ordinary interests, guiding one's actions and thoughts towards a higher purpose or divine principle. In the spiritual context, devotion is not only about the acts of worship or rituals but encompasses a comprehensive lifestyle and mindset that prioritizes spiritual growth and connection.

Understanding the Essence of Devotion

At its heart, devotion is characterized by a passionate enthusiasm or love for something greater than oneself. This could be devotion to a deity, a set of spiritual teachings, or a path of personal transformation. It is an intense and committed relationship that shapes how one interacts with the world. Devotion infuses one's actions with purpose and imbues everyday activities with deeper significance, making the mundane aspects of life richer and more meaningful.

Devotion in a spiritual sense often involves practices such as prayer, meditation, studying sacred texts, or engaging in religious ceremonies. However, it extends beyond these practices to influence one's ethical decisions, interpersonal relationships, and self-concept. It is a force that orients a person towards the divine or the sacred, leading them to act with integrity and compassion.

Cultivating Spiritual Devotion

Developing a strong sense of devotion requires intentional practice and discipline. It begins with defining one's spiritual goals and understanding what one is devoted to. This clarity is crucial as it guides all subsequent actions and decisions. Once a clear sense of spiritual direction is established, one can begin to integrate practices that support this devotion into daily life.

Regular spiritual practices, such as meditation, prayer, or chanting, are fundamental for nurturing devotion. These practices help to keep the object of devotion at the forefront of one's mind, reinforcing commitment and deepening spiritual connection. They create a routine that becomes a sacred space for reflection and connection, crucial for sustaining long-term devotion.

Engaging with a community that shares similar spiritual goals can also significantly enhance one's devotion. Community provides support, accountability, and inspiration. It offers a network of like-minded individuals who can offer guidance, share in spiritual practices, and provide encouragement during challenging times. This communal aspect of devotion is often instrumental in maintaining enthusiasm and commitment.

Challenges in Sustaining Devotion

Maintaining spiritual devotion over a long period can be challenging. Life's distractions, changes in personal circumstances, and even periods of doubt and spiritual dryness can diminish one's fervor. The commercialism and materialism prevalent in modern society can also pull individuals away from their spiritual commitments, making superficial appeals to convenience and immediate gratification.

Moreover, devotion requires a balance between one's spiritual practices and the demands of everyday life. Finding this balance can be difficult, especially when faced with the pressures and responsibilities of family, work, and social obligations.

Integrating Devotion into Everyday Life

To effectively integrate devotion into daily life, it is helpful to see every action as an opportunity to express one's spiritual values. This might involve offering acts of kindness, making ethical choices, or simply being fully present in the moment. Such an approach allows devotion to permeate all aspects of life, rather than being confined to explicit spiritual practices.

Furthermore, setting aside specific times for spiritual reflection and practice is crucial. These moments can serve as daily reminders of one's spiritual commitments and help to strengthen and renew one's focus.

The Role of Teachings and Mentors

Spiritual teachings and mentors play a crucial role in deepening devotion. Teachings provide the philosophical foundation and practical guidance necessary for navigating the spiritual path, while mentors offer personal insights, encouragement, and examples of devoted living. Engaging deeply with teachings and seeking mentorship can enrich one's understanding and enhance the sincerity of one's devotion.

Living with Devotion

Living a life of devotion transforms existence into a continuous spiritual journey. Every experience, challenge, and joy becomes an opportunity to grow, learn, and connect more deeply with the spiritual dimensions of life. This approach to living ensures that one's spiritual commitments remain vibrant and dynamic, rather than static or ritualistic.

Devotion is a powerful aspect of spiritual life that enriches one's existence and deepens one's connection to the divine. It involves a committed practice, a supportive community, and the integration of spiritual principles into every aspect of life. By cultivating and sustaining devotion, individuals gain a profound source of strength, guidance, and purpose, enhancing both their own lives and those of others around them.

ᐅᐅᐅ

"Devotion is the melody of the spirit sung through daily acts of love and faithfulness. It is the deep current beneath the surface of life, guiding us gently towards our divine purpose."

ᐁᐁᐁ

EIGHTEEN

BALANCE: HARMONIZING MIND, BODY, AND SPIRIT

Balance is a fundamental concept in many spiritual and holistic health traditions, emphasizing the importance of achieving harmony among the mind, body, and spirit. This holistic approach suggests that true well-being comes from caring for all aspects of oneself, ensuring that each part is healthy and functioning well in concert with the others. This interconnectedness not only enhances personal health and happiness but also contributes to one's ability to live a full and productive life.

Understanding the Interconnection of Mind, Body, and Spirit

The mind, body, and spirit are deeply interconnected, each influencing the others in profound ways. The mind can affect physical health through stress, which can lead to physical symptoms and diseases; the body can affect mental health through hormonal balances and physical activity, which influence mood and cognitive functions; and the spirit—or one's sense of purpose and connection—can affect overall health by providing a sense of peace and fulfillment that buffers against mental stress and physical illness.

Recognizing this interdependence is the first step in achieving balance. It involves understanding how emotions, thoughts, physical health, and spiritual well-being can be aligned to promote overall health and well-being. This balance is dynamic, requiring continuous attention and adjustment as circumstances change.

Practices to Enhance Balance

Several practices can help individuals achieve and maintain balance among the mind, body, and spirit. These practices often involve elements of self-care that foster health in each area.

Meditation and Mindfulness: These practices support mental and spiritual health by helping to calm the mind, reduce stress, and increase self-awareness and presence. Meditation can also have physical benefits, such as reducing blood pressure and improving immune function.

Regular Physical Activity: Exercise is crucial for maintaining physical health but also benefits mental health by reducing symptoms of depression and anxiety. Physical activities that also incorporate mindfulness, such as yoga or tai chi, can additionally support spiritual well-being by fostering a deeper connection to the body and present moment.

Nutritious Diet: What one eats significantly affects physical health, but it can also impact mental clarity and emotional stability. A diet rich in fruits, vegetables, whole grains, and lean proteins can enhance physical health while also supporting stable mood and energy levels.

Adequate Rest: Sleep is fundamental to both mental and physical health. A regular sleep schedule not only rejuvenates the body and mind but also supports emotional stability and spiritual clarity by providing the energy needed for reflection and meditation.

Connection and Community: Engaging with a supportive community can enhance spiritual health, which in turn benefits mental and physical health. Being part of a community provides a sense of belonging and support, which are crucial for emotional well-being.

Challenges to Maintaining Balance

Achieving balance is often easier said than done. Modern life is filled with demands that can pull individuals in multiple directions, often prioritizing one aspect of health at the expense of others. For example, professional obligations can lead to stress and physical inactivity, while neglecting spiritual practices.

Furthermore, each person's needs are unique, and what constitutes balance for one individual may be different for another. Finding and maintaining this personal balance requires ongoing self-reflection and adaptation.

Integrating Balance into Daily Life

To effectively integrate balance into daily life, it's important to develop routines that incorporate practices supporting mind, body, and spirit. This might include setting aside specific times for meditation, scheduling regular exercise, planning meals that nourish the body, and making time for social interactions and personal reflection.

It is also helpful to periodically reassess one's lifestyle and make adjustments as needed. Life changes, such as a new job, a move, or a change in health, can all affect one's balance and require modifications to one's routine.

Living with Balance

Living a balanced life enhances one's ability to cope with life's challenges and contributes to a more fulfilling existence. By nurturing the mind, body, and spirit, individuals can enjoy better health, improved relationships, and a deeper sense of satisfaction.

Balance is not a static state but a continuous journey. It requires commitment, awareness, and flexibility as one navigates the complexities of life. By striving for harmony among the mind, body, and spirit, individuals can enhance their health, deepen their relationships, and live more purposefully and peacefully.

ᐅᐅᐅ

"Balance is not something you find, but something
you create. It is the delicate harmony of mind, body,
and spirit achieved through conscious choices and
sustained effort."

▷▷▷

NINETEEN

TRANSFORMATION: THE JOURNEY OF PERSONAL EVOLUTION

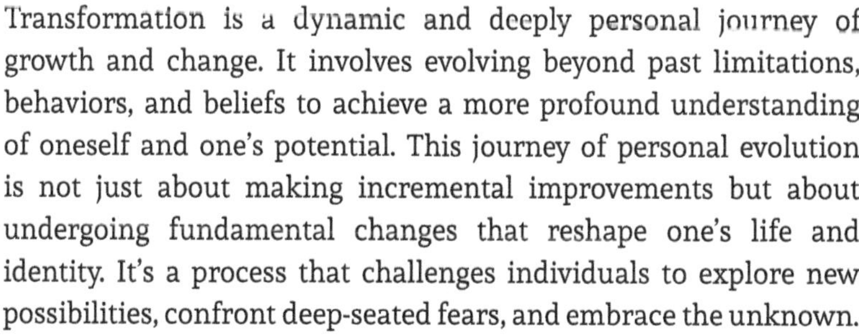

Transformation is a dynamic and deeply personal journey of growth and change. It involves evolving beyond past limitations, behaviors, and beliefs to achieve a more profound understanding of oneself and one's potential. This journey of personal evolution is not just about making incremental improvements but about undergoing fundamental changes that reshape one's life and identity. It's a process that challenges individuals to explore new possibilities, confront deep-seated fears, and embrace the unknown.

Understanding the Nature of Transformation

Transformation involves significant shifts in how individuals see themselves and the world around them. It can be triggered by various factors, such as a major life event, a deep personal crisis, or a sudden insight that changes everything. Regardless of the trigger, transformation often begins with a period of introspection and self-examination, where old values and assumptions are questioned, and new perspectives begin to emerge.

This process often requires confronting uncomfortable truths about oneself, such as unacknowledged weaknesses, buried emotions, or neglected aspirations. It also involves shedding behaviors and thought patterns that no longer serve one's best interests or align with one's evolving goals. This shedding process is often accompanied by a sense of loss, which can be painful yet is essential for making room for new growth.

Stages of Transformation

The journey of transformation can be viewed through various models, but many include stages such as awakening, purging, and rebirth:

Awakening: This stage involves a growing awareness of new possibilities and often begins with a feeling of restlessness or dissatisfaction with one's current state. It might be triggered by an event, a piece of knowledge, or an encounter that challenges existing beliefs and inspires a desire for change.

Purging: As individuals delve deeper into their transformation, they often go through a phase of purging old habits, relationships, and beliefs that are no longer in alignment with their new path. This stage is about clearing out what no longer serves the evolving self, which can be both liberating and challenging.

Rebirth: Rebirth is the stage where individuals begin to fully embrace their new identity and the changes they have undergone. It involves integrating new insights and practices into one's life and starting to live in accordance with the new self. This stage is characterized by a renewed sense of purpose and often a new direction in life.

The Role of Support in Transformation

Transformation is rarely a solitary journey. Support from others who understand or have experienced similar changes can be invaluable. This support can come from friends, family, mentors, or a community of individuals who are on or have gone through their own transformational journeys. Support groups and therapists can also play crucial roles, providing a safe space to explore difficult emotions and experiences.

Challenges Along the Transformational Journey

Transformation is inherently challenging. It requires enduring the discomfort of leaving the familiar behind and facing the uncertainties of new ways of being. Fear of the unknown, fear of failure, and even fear of success can all surface during this process. Overcoming these fears requires courage, persistence, and resilience.

Additionally, transformation often involves periods of confusion and disorientation, sometimes referred to as the "dark night of the soul," where old patterns have been shed, but new patterns have not yet fully formed. Navigating this phase can be particularly difficult because it can feel like one is in a liminal space between the old self and the new.

Integrating Changes into Everyday Life

To make transformation enduring, changes need to be integrated into everyday life. This might involve adopting new habits, cultivating new relationships, or changing one's environment to support the new self. It also involves continuous reflection and adjustment as one learns more about the nuances of their evolving identity and life path.

Living Transformed

Ultimately, living a transformed life means embodying the changes that have been made and continuing to grow in alignment with one's deepest values and aspirations. It involves being open to continuous learning and evolution, recognizing that transformation is not a finite process but an ongoing journey of personal development.

The journey of personal transformation is one of the most profound and challenging experiences an individual can undertake. It requires courage, commitment, and resilience but offers significant rewards, including a deeper understanding of oneself, a more authentic life, and the ability to contribute more fully to the world. By embracing the transformative process, individuals can achieve remarkable personal growth and find lasting fulfillment.

ᗡᗡᗡ

"Transformation is the continuous journey of the
soul towards enlightenment. It demands everything
of us, offering in return the boundless freedom of
our full potential."

ɒɒɒ

TWENTY

INTEGRITY IN ACTION: APPLYING PRINCIPLES IN DAILY LIFE

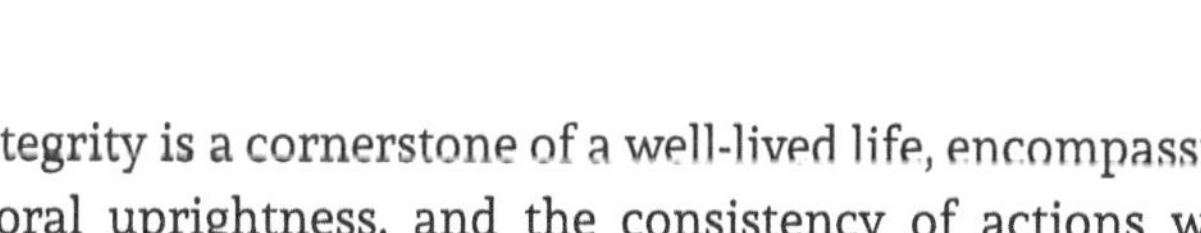

Integrity is a cornerstone of a well-lived life, encompassing honesty, moral uprightness, and the consistency of actions with avowed values and principles. It is not just a passive attribute but an active extension of one's ethical beliefs into everyday actions. Integrity in action means making choices that are not only legally right but are also morally commendable, living a life that is transparent and consistent across all situations, irrespective of whether one is being observed or not.

Understanding Integrity

Integrity involves adherence to a code of ethical values such as honesty, respect, and fairness. It implies the wholeness of character, with actions, words, and beliefs aligned in harmony. When one acts with integrity, decisions are predictably consistent with stated beliefs, and actions follow naturally from one's ethical convictions.

Acting with integrity requires courage and resilience, as it often means doing what is right even when it is not convenient, profitable, or popular. This might mean standing up for a disadvantaged colleague, admitting an error that could have serious repercussions, or opting out of a lucrative deal that doesn't align with one's ethical standards.

The Challenges of Maintaining Integrity

One of the primary challenges of integrity is that it often requires making tough decisions that might go against one's short-term interests or the expectations of others. In the professional realm, for example, maintaining integrity can mean foregoing immediate gains to preserve one's long-term reputation and self-respect. In personal relationships, it might involve being honest about one's feelings or actions, even when it might cause temporary pain or conflict.

Moreover, integrity demands constant vigilance. In a world where ethical lines can sometimes seem blurred, maintaining a clear sense of right and wrong, and adhering strictly to those standards, can be challenging. The pressure to conform to less stringent ethical norms can be strong, particularly if surrounding peers or society generally espouse more flexible moral positions.

Cultivating Integrity in Everyday Life

To cultivate integrity, one must first define their core values clearly. This might involve introspection and possibly discussion with trusted mentors or advisors to determine what principles are non-negotiable and which might be subject to change under certain circumstances.

Once these values are established, they must be integrated

consistently into daily decision-making processes. This integration can be facilitated by setting up systems and habits that encourage ethical behavior. For instance, one might decide to regularly reflect on their actions at the end of the day to evaluate whether they acted in accordance with their values and where they might improve.

Education and continuous learning about ethical principles and their application in various scenarios also support the maintenance of integrity. This ongoing education can help clarify one's understanding of complex moral issues and provide guidance on how to handle them.

Examples of Integrity in Action

Integrity can manifest in many ways, depending on the context:

In the workplace, it might involve giving credit to others for their contributions, providing honest feedback, or admitting to mistakes rather than covering them up.

In personal relationships, acting with integrity can involve being truthful and faithful, even in small matters.

In public life, integrity might involve standing by one's principles even when doing so may result in personal or professional backlash.

The Impact of Living with Integrity

Living a life marked by integrity can have profound impacts on both the individual and their community. For the individual, it fosters a deep sense of self-respect and inner peace, knowing that one's actions are consistent with their beliefs. It can also enhance relationships, as others learn that one is trustworthy and dependable.

For the community, the impact of seeing integrity in action can be inspirational and transformational. It sets a standard for ethical behavior that can elevate the conduct of an entire group, be it a family, a workplace, a community, or even a nation.

Integrating Integrity into One's Lifestyle

Living with integrity means more than just occasional ethical decisions; it involves a lifestyle of consistent ethical living. It requires awareness and careful consideration of the ethical dimensions of everyday choices and a commitment to live accordingly.

Integrity in action is about consistently applying one's ethical principles in daily life. It requires clarity of values, commitment to ethical behavior, and the courage to uphold one's standards, even when it is difficult. This commitment to living with integrity not only enriches one's life but also contributes to building a more ethical and just society.

ﭏﭏﭏ

"Integrity in action is the manifestation of our deepest convictions; it is living proof that what we believe profoundly influences the world around us. It is the quiet yet unmistakable power of a life lived with unwavering authenticity."

Citation And References

This book represents the culmination of extensive research and meticulous analysis, incorporating a diverse range of sources, including numerous books, scholarly studies, and personal experiences. Additionally, I have scoured various websites to gather relevant information and data essential for the compilation of this work. I have taken every precaution to ensure the accuracy of the information presented and have diligently cited all sources to acknowledge their contributions.

Despite these efforts, the possibility of inadvertent errors remains. I deeply value the insights of my readers and appreciate any feedback that can help identify and rectify such inaccuracies. I encourage you to bring any discrepancies to my attention.

Your feedback is not only welcome but crucial, as it will aid in correcting current editions and enhancing the content of future ones. I am committed to maintaining the highest standards of accuracy and reliability in my work and thank you for your support and understanding.

Additionally, I firmly uphold the principle of freedom of speech and expression as guaranteed under Article 19(1)(a) of the Constitution of India, and I respect the diverse viewpoints and expressions of all readers.

ppp

Other Books Of The Author

1. Empowering Minds: A Journey into Women's Self-Discovery and Power
2. The Dynamics of Motivation: Catalyzing Thought into Action
3. Meditation and Mental Well Being: The Path to Inner Peace and Clarity
4. The Psychology of Child Education: Nurturing Future Generations
5. Ethical Enlightenment: A Modern Guide to Living with Integrity
6. Voices of Empowerment: Stories of Women Rising Against Odds
7. Social Psychology in Everyday Life: Understanding Human Connections
8. The Essence of Motivational Speaking: Inspiring Change in Others
9. Balancing Acts: Women, Work, and the Will to Lead
10. Guiding with Grace: Raising Children with Compassion and Awareness
11. The Power of Positive Aging: Embracing Life After Fifty
12. Building Resilient Communities: Social Work in Action
13. The Ethical Educator: Principles for Teaching and Learning
14. From Insight to Impact: Social Psychology for a Better World
15. The Ethics of Empathy: A Guide to Ethical Living
16. The Science of Empowering the Self: Navigating Life's Challenges with Psychological Wisdom
17. The Mindful Conscious Leader: Meditation Techniques for Modern Management
18. Pioneering Spirit: Women's Pathways to Leadership and Empowerment
19. Feeling to Healing: The Role of Emotional Intelligence in Child Development
20. Transformative Talks and Words of Inspiration: Insights into Motivational Oratory

❧❧❧

Contact

Dr. Minakshi Bansal
Social Activist
Ahmedabad, Gujarat, Bharat
minakshiindiag20@yahoo.com

❧❧❧

|| LOKAHA SAMASTHAHA SUKHINO BHAVANTU ||

● 127 ●